God's Providence

The Gift of Adoption

by

Cee Mystique

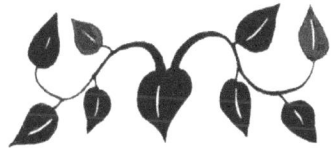

Copyright © 2020 by Cee Mystique

All rights reserved. No part of this publication may be reproduced, stored or introduced into a retrieval system, or transmitted in any form, or by any means, (electronic, mechanical, photocopying, recording or otherwise), without the prior written permission of the publisher or the author.

www.MystiqueJournals.com

Book Cover and Layout design by Virginia Cantarella

ISBN Hardcover: 978-978-1-7336697-0-2 Limited Edition Print
ISBN Paperback: 978-978-1-7336697-1-9
ISBN eBook: 978-978-1-7336697-2-6

Table of Contents

Acknowledgments	p. iv
Preface	p. vi
Chapter 1	p. 1
Chapter 2	p. 3
Chapter 3	p. 5
Chapter 4	p. 7
Chapter 5	p. 8
Chapter 6	p. 10
Chapter 7	p. 12
Conclusion	p. 13
Author's Note	p. 14
Some Adoption Resources	p. 15
Scripture References	p.16
Bibliography	p. 18
Future Books by the Author	p. 19

"Each child belongs to all of us and they will bring us a tomorrow in direct relation to the responsibility we have shown to them."
Maya Angelou

Acknowledgments

This book is truly a gift of love from above. After writing four novels with the desire to have the first book released two years ago by my birthday, I remained steadfast in believing one day they would be released. Over the past two years, I have learned lessons and developed new skills to prepare me for this moment. This journey didn't take place in solitude but with supportive family and friends whose encouragement and belief in my writing fueled my determination to Never to Give Up!

To my big brother, Winston, whose words always encourage, affirm, and inspire me to strive, especially when he sees more in me than I see in myself. To my sisters, Regina & Brandy, who laugh, cry, correct, and build me up through every twist and turn life throws at me. I say thank you for believing in me and pushing me to see and do more for myself.

After speaking with my Heavenly Father, I seek two types of clarity, spiritual and practical, mostly if my communication resulted in implementation. From the first day we met till now, Terryl has always provided that practical roadmap. Thank you for helping me stay focused and clear on my mission, cutting through the forest to find my yellow brick road.

Then there are those whose entrance into your life seems segmented to a particular area, but time shows how their lives entwined wonderfully with yours. The next two ladies have woven their fabric around my heart and created a bond that I will forever cherish, Mara and her beautiful mother, Virginia. Mara has walked with me through many challenges with my boys' care, supported my company's mission, and continued to encourage my writings from my blogs to my novels. When I shared my progress with this book, Mara introduced me to Virginia, who, after a few conversations, I asked Mara if she could adopt me as her sister. Virginia not only offered to create the beautiful cover for this book but, with a mother's love of questioning and guidance, has walked me through the cover to the final formatting. For this, I am forever grateful.

If God had told me all the beautiful friendships I would have made from placing my son in residential school, I would have doubted it. But I have made some lifelong friendships that will live past my son's departure. One such relationship has allowed me front row privilege of watching God work in and through her life. For without our bond, this book would not have existed. Thank you Meagan, for letting me into your life and trusting me to share your story, a story I am sure will touch and help other women who desire to be a mother but struggle with the natural process of things.

To my friends mentioned and those not that continue to support my dreams, thank you.

It may not happen when and how one thinks it should, but never give up on your dreams of soaring on eagle wings.

Cee Mystique

Preface

Many young girls grow up with the desire to become a mother. Some want a houseful of children while others may want only one or two.

As young women grow up, their lives often take them down different paths than their childhood dreams could have imagined.

For some, pregnancies come easy; there are no medical, sociological, and economic barriers hindering or preventing these women's path to motherhood. They grow up, may or may not get married, and have their children.

However, the path may not be as simple or straightforward for others. Let me tell you a story about three such women whose paths to motherhood is forever entwined.

The Believing Mom

The Believing Mom desired to have children through marriage. Yet, struggling through life's ups and downs, various health issues, and her first marriage's dissolution left her questioning if children would happen. Then, God blessed her with her second husband, and during their third year of marriage, they receive a prophecy of the blessing of twins. During the fifth year of marriage, they conceived their first child, but Believing Mom, unfortunately, miscarried during the first trimester for unknown medical reasons. Through this trial, God gave clarity on her calling, purpose, mission, and the promise of His word. Later that year, in full belief, she conceived and gave birth to her first son.

The Praying Mom

As a young woman who loved children since her own childhood, Praying Mom dreamed of having children of her own one day. However, growing up near power plants that emitted cancerous gases which created unhealthy environmental conditions left Praying Mom plagued by reproductive health issues. Despite her sickness, she continued to pray to God to bless her so that she might hold children of her own. With her dream still unfulfilled, she found herself married and working in a residential school, teaching special needs children and loving them as her own.

The Sacrificing Mom

For various reasons, some young women cannot fully take on the mantle of motherhood. Upon finding out that they are pregnant, some make a tremendous gift of love.

Here is their story…

Chapter 1

Believing Mom gave birth to her first son during the sixth year of her marriage. Hers was a high-risk pregnancy because of the miscarriage she suffered earlier in the year. From the second month of her son's pregnancy, her bundle of joy gave the doctors reason to pause, and that placed Believing Mom on a biweekly appointment schedule throughout her entire pregnancy.

Believing Mom knew the God she served was faithful and just, and that His word never returns to Him without accomplishing that which He said He would do.[1] That summer, she gave birth to a healthy 8.8 pound beautiful baby boy who was one inch shy of two feet long. She loved her son immediately, but her concern began growing while still in the delivery room. He could not latch onto the breast or a bottle nipple.

The doctors explained her baby was born with low muscle tone within his facial structure, creating the complication of failing to suck. The lactation specialist worked with her son each day, using various techniques and tricks to strengthen the baby's jaw muscles. On his one-week check-up, after a week of struggling with strict breastfeeding and after documenting the drastic drop of weight, the pediatrician diagnosed her son with "failure to thrive." The matter was resolved by purchasing a breast pump and adding baby formula into his diet.

Over the next few months, however, various other medical issues slowly arose in her son. At seven months, the baby suffered from a severe upper respiratory infection. This infection affected his airways, nose, and throat, requiring a double dose of antibiotics over fourteen days to enable him to recover. Believing Mom's once singing, smiling, talkative, bubbly little boy was now just a shell of himself. Believing Mom found herself faced with a gut-wrenching diagnosis. The extreme respiratory infection uncovered hidden issues which led her son's diagnosis of regressive autism. Although he had seemed to develop as a typical baby, he now was losing speech and social abilities.

Over the next ten years, Believing Mom gave birth to her second son, earned her college degree, found herself divorced again, and followed her passion to become an author of women issues. She also realized, like Hannah from the Bible, that she needed to send her firstborn to be raised in a "House of Eli." [2] She believed that God would direct her to a residential school that would provide her oldest with the twenty-four care he now required to grow into the man God created him to be. Believing Mom spent many days and nights in prayer and fasting for direction to find the proper placement for her son.

Chapter 2

Nearly 300 miles away, Praying Mom was a paraprofessional in a residential school up in the mountains. Her love for children had led her down a career path dedicated to teaching precious special needs children to live as independently as they possibly could. She loved her job, her husband, and her life. The only thing missing was a little child to call her own. Over the years, she suffered medical issues, including a diagnosis of endometriosis and ovarian cancer, which began the trials and tribulations of her reproduction system and having children.

As fate would have it, Believing Mom found her way to place her son in a school in the mountains. Though the school was nearly 300 miles away, she knew in her heart this was "The House of Eli" God had destined for him to attend. The house where he would be staying was called Cedar 2, signifying the spiritual meaning of protection. She saw this as a sign that her son would be safe, sheltered, and secured. As she left her son in his new home, she rested on God's peace returning home as her mother's heart cried on the inside because of the separation.

Praying Mom had bouts of sickness that would cause her to be in and out of work, but God continued to hear her cry in prayer and healed her. She held on to the hope in prayer that she would have a child.

Eight years after her cancer treatment with radioactive iodine, Praying Mom suffered a miscarriage during the ninth week of her first pregnancy. Diagnosed with endometriosis, doctors ignored Praying Mom's questions and fears concerning her past medication as she hemorrhaged for three months. It was the fifth doctor she saw who saved her life and changed her life's direction through God's grace. The doctor listened to the family's concerns and, through a battery of tests, diagnosed Praying Mom with von Willebrand disease (VWD), a blood disorder inherited from her father. The doctor also informed Praying Mom that she had several concerning tumors within her uterus.

After the first year, the care manager assigned to Believing Mom's son resigned to pursue a position in her degree. As God would have it, Praying Mom was promoted and appointed as the new care manager for Believing Mom's son. Over time, their acquaintance grew into a true friendship. As each of them went through their challenges, they would pray for each other no matter what the situation, whether it be for Believing Mom's son or other challenges affecting the women's family or health.

At the end of her first year as care manager, Praying Mom took a medical leave of absence that lasted through the beginning of the following year. She underwent at least three surgeries to remove the tumors. Because of the tumors' placement within the uterus and their size, Praying Mom's surgery required the removal of part of her uterus, one fallopian tube, and one ovary. Nevertheless, she continued praying to have a child of her own one day, even though it would be a high-risk pregnancy if she conceived. There was also the fact that under no condition could she go into labor, her doctor informed her, in fear that she could bleed out.

Chapter 3

 Believing Mom needed major reproductive surgery during the third year of her son's residency. For years, Believing Mom suffered from various issues that affected her reproductive system. She shared this info with Praying Mom, who in turn shared her medical issues over the years and her dreams of having children of her own. Believing Mom understood Praying Mom's desire and need to have children since she herself had been thirty-six years old before finally giving birth to her first child. But Believing Mom also understood the risks Praying Mom would be putting her body through to bring a precious life into this world. So she prayed and asked God to help Praying Mom see that her motherhood path may not follow her childhood dreams.
 Thanks be to God! Believing Mom came through her hysterectomy with little pain and fast recovery. Believing Mom praised God for her healing and thanked her friends, who all had given her advice on preparing for the surgery and taking care of herself afterwards.
 At this time, Believing Mom was also penning her first sequel and had just finished writing one of the climatic scenes before visiting her son in the mountains. Believing Mom always enjoyed her visits with him. She got to see his growth in skills since her last visit, take in the beauty of God's glory in the open field, and spend time with the friends she has made at school, especially Praying Mom.
 During this visit, Praying Mom shared she was again going through blood transfusions, chemotherapy, and uterine tumors, and how she wasn't willing to give up hope of having children of her own. Believing Mom once more sympathized with Praying Mom, however, she wanted to help

Praying Mom understand some fundamental truths. She asked Praying Moms some questions. "Do you love your husband? Does your husband genuinely love you? Are you being fair to him by putting your life in danger to give birth to a child? Would it be fair to give him a child to raise alone, knowing he may have to bury you?"

    Then God reminded Believing Mom of a passage she had written in her story, one which spoke to the internal battle Praying Mom was facing. Believing Mom explained that motherhood comes in many forms. Some couples have a host mother who carries the child, conceived by both mother and father, in her uterus; such was the passage to motherhood for Gabriel Union. She shared that others follow the steps of Viola Davis, Jamie Lee Curtis, Diane Keaton, and many others who opened their home and heart to children through adoption. No matter which way God intended to answer Praying Mom's prayer to motherhood, He needed her to understand that her life was more valuable and that He loved her. He needed her to see that her husband loved her, and that she must rethink her priorities, including what was most important to her husband, her family and, even more, to the child, if, God forbid, she died during childbirth. After Believing Mom returned home, she sent Praying Mom a passage from her unreleased book to hear a love petition from a male perspective.

Chapter 4

Over the next couple of months, Believing Mom and Praying Mom stayed in contact professionally and socially, sharing the highs and the lows of their lives. At the beginning of the year, Praying Mom shared that she and her husband had decided to adopt children as they were in a good place and her health was stable. Life was good in both homes at this point. Then a global pandemic hit the world. Believing Mom was grateful that she and her youngest son had seen her oldest son at the beginning of March before each state locked their borders. Unfortunately, Believing Mom and Praying Mom weren't able to connect during that visit, but they stayed in contact.

In the middle of the COVID-19 madness, life continued. Praying Mom and her husband moved forward with the requirements to become adoptive parents. Believing Mom and Praying Mom received more explosive news on June 23. The school in which God had placed Believing Mom's oldest son and where Praying Mom worked would be closing in five months. Not an easy pill to swallow for anyone, but Believing Mom knew God was in control. She was not sure how things would work out, but she knew they would.

As time went on, Praying Mom's sister gave birth to a little boy. As she shared in the family joy, she also shared with Believing Mom her sadness of not having her own baby. Believing Mom reminded her that God hears and knew her desires, and at the appointed time, He would bless her.

Chapter 5

In late August, Praying Mom's health changed. She found herself in the emergency room facing the diagnosis of being out of remission. For the next couple of weeks, Praying Mom returned to chemotherapy and was told she would need to have a total hysterectomy at this time. The news devastated her.

During a conversation with Believing Mom, Praying Mom was reminded that everything has a reason. Though this was another difficult pill to swallow, and amid COVID-19, God was still in charge. Plus, it was better to have this procedure done now than after she adopted her child.

While both Believing Mom and Praying Mom were praying for resolution regarding the school closing and Praying Mom's health, Sacrificing Mother was having a crisis of her own.

We may never know Sacrificing Mom's back story. What we do know is this young lady found herself pregnant with a child she could not raise. Many times, society looks down on unwed mothers, calling them promiscuous or loose. But the fact remains that some young ladies may find themselves with a child from a violent act committed against them. It is also possible for women who have used full protection to find themselves with an ill-timed or unwanted pregnancy. Often, people scorn women who have children out of wedlock, have aborted a child, or have brought a child into the world without the financial means to raise him or her. Many factors could have led Sacrificing Mom to where she was at this moment.

Sacrificing Mom did not believe in abortion, so we know she cherished the life of the baby she carried in her womb. However, she knew that she would not be able to take on the mantle of motherhood. Sacrificing Mom wanted her precious bundle of joy to have a life better than she was able to provide. So with the desire to give her child the world, Sacrificing Mom decided to place her infant up for adoption. Sacrificing Mom kept herself safe and healthy during her pregnancy, loving and caring for the gift of life growing within her.

Chapter 6

On the morning of August 31, Believing Mom sent an email to the transitioning team responsible for finding a new placement for her oldest child which simply stated, "What is the Department of Education's next list of schools to apply to? With less than sixty days, I am praying that God has a ram in the bush!" [3] Believing Mom had continually prayed over this matter for each school the Lord had orchestrated for either of her sons attended, and she expected God to continue to do the same now.

That night, Praying Mom, her co-workers, Believing Mom, and the rest of the remaining students received the gifted ram! Another organization stepped forward to save the school and the campus. From the West Coast to the East Coast, from North to South, parents and staff alike were grateful for such a gift. Over the next couple of weeks, the incoming CEO introduced himself to the employees and parents, calming the nerves and worries of parents who, like Believing Mom, could not find a new placement for their children. Believing Mom thanked God and asked Him to bless the staff that remained under the new leadership, especially all those who cared for her son in her absence.

However, Praying Mom's health was getting worse. She was hospitalized for losing an excessive amount of blood and suffering fainting spells, so her hysterectomy was scheduled for October. Believing Mom and Praying Mom talked or texted many days during this time. Believing Mom, having gone through this surgery just two years earlier, tried to squash many of Praying Mom's fears. Believing Mom wanted Praying

Mom to keep her mind off the loss of her childhood dream; God was preparing to bless her within time, but now she only needed to concern herself with getting healthy and strong.

Chapter 7

On September 14, Praying Mom was admitted to the hospital for excessive hemorrhaging and passing of tissue. The doctors gave her a blood transfusion to stabilized her and changed the surgery from October to the earliest time the surgical team could be assembled. On the same night, Sacrificing Mom was admitted into the maternity ward, and her precious son with strawberry-blonde hair was born.

At 6:00 a.m. on September 23, while Praying Mom was being prepped for surgery, Believing Mom was saying her weekly prayer. She requested the saints to lifted Praying Mom in worship to the throne room of our Heavenly Father, asking the blood of Jesus to cover the surgery. The morning would also prove personally challenging for Believing Mom as well, but God sent her an assignment to focus on rather than the personal challenges the morning had delivered.

Also on this morning, Sacrificing Mom needed to finalize her decision to place her son up for adoption, and she was looking through the prospective parents' bios for the perfect family to care for her son. I would love to say her choice was made on their values and beliefs, or maybe the reference letters and the bio of the mother alone, but, alas, we may never know. Yet, while the surgeons were removing all hope of Praying Mom's chance of ever becoming a mother naturally, Sacrificing Mom studied Praying Mom's picture, which displayed her strawberry-blonde hair, and chose her as the woman to raise her son.

Conclusion

Only God could have had stars collide in such a way on September 14 and again on September 23. Only God could change a loss into a divine blessing!

The Scripture tells us that God has a plan for each of our lives[4] and that He knows us in the secrecy of our mother's womb.[5] The challenges we face daily are only a surprise to us, but the God of Abraham, Isaac, and Jacob is the same God who sits high and comes low to guide us today.[6]

Authors Note

This story was supposed to be a short blog to share God's providence with my readers to remind them that God hears our prayers and sees our tears; that every triumph or trial will work together according to the plan of God.[7]

As we find ourselves in various situations, we often question why, wondering how any good thing could come from our pain and tears. But the creator of heaven and earth does not think as we do.[8] Sometimes it doesn't make sense why certain events happen around or to us, but everything, no matter if it seems good or bad, wrong or right, will all work in our favor as long as God is in control.

In this story, God aligned the paths of three mothers. None of them knew their lives would cross or even why they presented themselves openly beyond the obvious reasons. But each mother had a divine mission to accomplish, set forth before the oldest of them was born. As defined by our country's legal system:

> Act of providence is an accident against which ordinary skill and foresight could not guard. This is synonymous to an act of God. For certain acts no one can be held responsible. Naturally occurring events that are unavoidable can be considered as act of providence.

Neither Believing Mom nor Sacrificing Mom knew their sons would be in the care of Praying Mom. And only God could have ordained the timing of when Sacrificing Mom would choose Praying Mom and sign the papers to coincide with the surgery's timing.

This story also highlights the gift of adoption. As reported by the Congressional Coalition on Adoption Institute, in the United States, "On any given day, over 437,000 children are living in the U.S. foster care system, and the number has been rising. Over 125,000 of these children are eligible for adoption, and they will wait, on average, four years for an adoptive family."

The report from the Adoption and Foster Care Analysis and Reporting states, as of September 2019, that 122,216 children handled by public welfare agencies are waiting to be adopted in the United States. Then there are the infants who are adopted more readily through private agencies. As noted in the story, there are many paths to motherhood. Adoption, however, is a path that leads to a gift that keeps on giving.

Some Adoption Resources

Adoption Network - adoptionnetork.com/

Gladney Center for Adoption – adoption.org

American Adoptions - americanadoptions.com

Scripture References

1. So also will be the word that I speak—it will not fail to do what I plan for it; it will do everything I send it to do. —Isaiah 55:11 GNT

2. After he was weaned, she took the boy with her, young as he was, along with a three-year-old bull, an ephah of flour and a skin of wine, and brought him to the house of the LORD at Shiloh. When the bull had been sacrificed, they brought the boy to Eli, and she said to him, "Pardon me, my LORD. As surely as you live, I am the woman who stood here beside you praying to the LORD. I prayed for this child, and the LORD has granted me what I asked of him. So now I give him to the LORD. For his whole life he will be given over to the LORD." And he worshiped the LORD there. — 1 Samuel 1:24-28 NIV

3. When they reached the place God had told him about, Abraham built an altar there and arranged the wood on it. He bound his son Isaac and laid him on the altar, on top of the wood. Then he reached out his hand and took the knife to slay his son. But the angel of the Lord called out to him from heaven, 'Abraham! Abraham!' 'Here I am,' he replied. 'Do not lay a hand on the boy,' he said. "Do not do anything to him. Now I know that you fear God, because you have not withheld from me your son, your only son.' Abraham looked up and there in a thicket he saw a ram caught by its horns. He went over and took the ram and sacrificed it as a burnt offering instead of his son. —Genesis 22:9-13 NIV

4. For I know the plans I have for you," declares the LORD, "plans to prosper you and not to harm you, plans to give you hope and a future. —Jeremiah 29:11 NIV

5. Before I formed you in the womb I knew you, before you were born I set you apart; I appointed you as a prophet to the nations. — Jeremiah 1:5 NIV

6. Though the LORD is highly exalted, yet he pays attention to those who are lowly regarded, but he is aware of the arrogant from afar. — Psalms 138:6 ISV

7. And we know that all things work together for good to those who love God, to those who are the called according to His purpose. —Romans 8:28 NKJV

8. The Lord says: "My thoughts and my ways are not like yours. Just as the heavens are higher than the earth, my thoughts and my ways are higher than yours. — Isaiah 55: 8-9 CEV

Bibliography

U.S. Department of Health and Human Services, Administration for Children and Families, Administration on Children, Youth and Families, Children's Bureau. "AFCARS Report #27". (August 24, 2020),
https://www.acf.hhs.gov/cb/resource/afcars-report-27.

Congressional Coalition on Adoption Institute, https://ccainstituteblog.org/

USLegal, "Act of Providence Law and Legal Definition", accessed October 21, 2020,
https://definitions.uslegal.com/a/act-of-providence/

Future Books by the Author

Future romance series, dealing with the hard issues women face in their life.

Matter of the Heart Series

Please join Cee Mystique Village at mystiquejournals.com to learn about all new books.

www.ingramcontent.com/pod-product-compliance
Lightning Source LLC
Chambersburg PA
CBHW021002090426
42736CB00010B/1430